X-Treme Sports

Rock Climbing

Kristin Van Cleaf

ABDO Publishing Company

visit us at
www.abdopub.com

Published by ABDO Publishing Company, 4940 Viking Drive, Edina, Minnesota 55435.
Copyright © 2003 by Abdo Consulting Group, Inc. International copyrights reserved in all countries. No part of this book may be reproduced in any form without written permission from the publisher.

Printed in the United States.

Cover Photo: Corbis
Interior Photos: Corbis pp. 4-5, 6, 7, 9, 11, 12, 13, 15, 17, 18, 19, 23, 24-25, 27, 29, 31

Editors: Kate A. Conley, Stephanie Hedlund, Jennifer R. Krueger
Art Direction: Neil Klinepier

Library of Congress Cataloging-in-Publication Data

Van Cleaf, Kristin, 1976-
  Rock climbing / Kristin Van Cleaf.
     p. cm. -- (X-treme sports)
  Includes index.
  Summary: Presents the history, needed equipment, and various techniques of rock climbing.
  ISBN 1-57765-930-9
  1. Rock climbing--Juvenile literature. [1. Rock climbing.] I. Title. II. Series.

GV200.2 V83 2003
796.52'23--dc21
                                       2002026096

Contents

Rock Climbing

Rock climbing has been described as ballet on rock. Climbers gracefully move up many types of rocks, cliffs, and even mountains. For some climbers, it is the destination that is important. For others, it is the path. But they all have one thing in common, a love of climbing.

Rock climbing began as part of mountain climbing. **Mountaineers** had to know how to hike, rock climb, and ice climb. To reach a mountaintop, they had to know how to anchor themselves to both rock and ice. They also needed to know how to find holds or make them.

Soon, people realized rock climbing was fun as its own activity. The sport took off, and equipment and **techniques** improved. Bouldering, sport climbing, ice climbing, and other forms of climbing soon developed. Today, people still enjoy the thrill of climbing rocks.

The Sport Begins

Climbing's earliest history begins with **mountaineering**. Mountaineers tried to tackle a mountain and reach its summit. In 1786, Frenchmen Michel-Gabriel Paccard and Jacques Balmat became the first people to reach the summit of Mont Blanc in the French Alps. At 15,771 feet (4,807 m), Mont Blanc is Europe's highest mountain.

After this first ascent, **mountaineers** began climbing to the highest, most difficult peaks. By the late 1800s, they had scaled most of Europe's major alpine peaks. Climbers then tackled more difficult routes on mountains that had already been climbed. Eventually, they began looking for peaks outside of Europe.

During the 1900s, different climbing standards developed. Many people still believed that reaching the mountain's summit was the goal of climbing. But the sport of rock climbing was slowly separating from mountaineering.

7

People slowly made improvements to rock climbing equipment and methods. After World War II, **surplus** army gear aided in the creation and improvement of safety gear. Protection devices and **nylon** rope soon appeared.

During the 1950s and 1960s, climbers in California's Yosemite Valley improved cliff climbing **techniques**. Climbers from around the world picked up these methods and modified them. Climbers now believed that grace and technique in climbing were just as rewarding as reaching the summit.

By the 1960s, rock climbing had been established as a separate sport. Throughout the 1960s and 1970s, new equipment developed. It included specialized rock climbing shoes, and protection devices. Ropes improved, furthering climbing safety.

In the 1980s, French climbers created new rock climbing methods, such as bouldering and sport climbing. These methods developed alongside traditional climbing. Soon, the use of indoor climbing walls increased. People began competing based on speed and difficulty. Today, climbers can choose the type of climbing they like best. It is a challenging sport enjoyed by people around the world.

Opposite page: This climber is bouldering.

Climbing Gear

Rock climbing involves a variety of gear. The climber does the work of moving up the rock. Rope, a harness, carabiners, and other gear keep the climber safe. With this gear, a person can climb without the fear of injury due to falling.

The rope is the climber's lifeline. It connects the climber to an anchor and catches the climber in a fall. Today's ropes are **nylon** kernmantle ropes. A kernmantle rope is a core of fibers wrapped in a sleeve of braided nylon. They come in different thicknesses and lengths.

Climbers use different knots to tie ropes to other items. However, they keep the main part of the rope free of knots and wear. Ropes are replaced regularly, depending on how often they are used.

The harness connects the climber to the rope. Harnesses are usually made of flat nylon webbing. Most of today's harnesses are a system of a belt and loops around the climber's waist and legs. This allows the climber to sit

*An oval carabiner and
a climbing rope*

comfortably in the harness. The sit design spreads out the pressure to protect the climber during a fall.

Carabiners are lightweight **aluminum** links. Carabiners made for rock climbing can hold a few thousand pounds. Climbers use carabiners to clip themselves to belay devices, anchors, and other gear. Carabiners can be one of several different shapes, but they all have a spring-loaded gate. Locking carabiners have gates that lock with a screw. They are usually used in belaying and rappelling.

Climbers also use devices to protect themselves from falls. These devices are called protection. They anchor the climber to the rock. The lead climber places the protection device in a crack in the rock. Then he or she wedges it in place.

Some protection devices have no moving parts. Chocks are an example of this. Chocks are nuts attached to short cables. Other protection devices have moving parts. They contract and then expand once placed in a crack. Friends are an example of

This climber is carrying carabiners, protection devices, and a bag of chalk.

this. Once a friend is placed in a crack, springs cause it to expand. This secures the friend in place.

Rock shoes are specially designed for rock climbing. The soles are made of sticky rubber that grips the rock. On long climbs, people often wear stiff-soled shoes. They provide support and allow a climber to stand on edges. People who climb on overhanging rocks often wear shoes with **flexible** soles to better feel the rock.

Rock climbers also wear helmets for safety in outdoor climbing. A helmet protects a climber's head from loose, falling rock. Rock climbing helmets are specially designed to allow free movement. They are usually made of plastic or **fiberglass**.

Climbers also use a variety of other equipment. They may use belay devices, slings, quickdraws, daypacks, and chalk. Climbers often carry food, water, and first aid supplies. They also dress properly for the weather. The type of equipment depends on the climb. Experienced climbers can help beginners choose the proper equipment.

Climbing Methods

Rock climbing is best learned from an instructor. Rock climbing clubs also introduce beginners to the basics of climbing and equipment. These clubs often set up outings and can help a beginner choose equipment and climbing locations.

Traditional climbing is done in pairs. The climber is on one end of a rope. The climber's partner, or belayer, is on the rope's other end. The belayer controls the amount of rope given to the climber. The belayer uses the rope to catch the climber in the event of a fall.

In traditional rock climbing, the rope can be secured in different ways. Beginners often top rope. With top roping, the rope feeds through an anchor at the top of the climb. The lead climber can also place protection devices in cracks as he or she climbs. At the top, the lead can then belay his or her partner, who becomes the second.

Some **techniques** make moving up the rock easier. Generally, it is best not to hug the rock. Climbing slightly away from the rock makes it easier to see footholds.

Climbing Commands

Climbing partners use signal words to communicate clearly with each other.

"On belay" means the climber is ready. When the belayer has his or her gear set, he or she will respond with "belay on."

"Climbing" tells the belayer the climber is beginning to climb. The belayer responds "climb."

"Slack" informs the belayer that the climber needs more rope.

"Watch me" tells the belayer to pay attention because the climber feels he or she may fall.

"Falling" means the climber is falling, so the belayer should put the rope in a brake position.

"Rock" tells those below that rock is falling. It should be repeated until the rock has stopped falling.

"Off belay" is the climber's signal that he or she has reached the top and is safe. The belayer responds "belay off" to confirm that the belay has ended.

Much of climbing involves the choice of foot and handholds. Be sure a hold is solid before using it. To save energy, choose holds with medium distances between them. Use your hands for balance, and do the actual climbing with your feet and legs. For safety, move one hand or foot at a time.

When pulling yourself up onto a hold, position the weight of your body over your feet. On some holds, it may help to turn your foot sideways. This is called edging. It places more of the shoe's sole on the rock for a better grip.

Climbers use their hands for support. A handhold uses the whole hand to grip the rock. Fingerholds involve hooking the fingers in small cracks and holes. Look for holds that may be right in front of your body, rather than higher up. This will keep your body balanced as you climb.

Experienced climbers can use other **techniques**, too. For example, they may use hand or foot jamming, chimneying, smearing, or traversing during difficult climbs. Many of these methods require experience and practice.

After climbing for long periods, a climber's legs may become tired and weak. To rest, find a solid ledge or foothold. Try lowering your heels below your toes. It may also help to straighten your legs. To prevent fatigue, plan each move. Try

not to shift your feet on a foothold more than necessary.

Once you have practiced the individual moves, try to climb smoothly. Moving your hands and feet in a rhythm makes climbing easier. It gives you **momentum** when moving up to each hold. Though it takes practice, setting a rhythm will help you save energy during a climb.

Returning to the ground can be tricky. A beginner who is top roping is often lowered to the ground by his or her belayer. A climber can also choose to climb back down. Facing out or sideways while descending may allow you to better see footholds.

Rappelling is another way to get down the rock. To do this, the climber leans back on the rope. The climber then slides down, guiding with his or her feet. This method is best learned from an instructor or other experienced climber.

Lingo

anchor

The anchor is a secure point to which the rope attaches.

belay

The belay keeps a climber from falling far by controlling the rope. The person controlling the rope is called the belayer.

daypack

A daypack holds a climber's gear.

hold

A hold is an edge of rock that a climber can grip with his or her hands or feet.

belay device

This device can be a metal ring with holes, or a figure eight-shaped piece. The rope threads through the device, allowing the belayer to apply pressure on the rope and stop a fall.

crash pad

This soft pad is placed beneath a climber indoors or outdoors for safety in a fall.

carabiner

A carabiner is a metal loop with a spring-loaded gate on one side. It is used to connect pieces of equipment.

bouldering

This type of climbing is done on low boulders. The routes are often short but difficult.

chimneying

In this technique, the climber uses his or her back, hands, and feet to slide up the inside of a wide crack.

traditional climbing

Traditional climbing usually involves a lead and a second climber. The lead places the protection devices while belayed by the second, who often removes the devices as he or she climbs.

lead

The lead, or lead climber, is the first person to climb. Often the lead places the protection devices, which can be used by the second.

protection

Protection devices anchor the climber to the rock for protection in case of a fall.

second

The second person to climb is called the second. Often, the belayer will become the second once the lead is safely at the top.

rack

A climber's rack is a sling that holds the climbing gear. It is also the gear a climber chooses to carry.

rappel

Rappelling is a method of descent. The climber slides down the rock on a rope, with his or her feet guiding the way.

jamming

Jamming involves wedging a hand, finger, or foot in a crack and using it to pull the body up.

free climbing

Free climbing involves using only the hands and feet on the rock. The climber uses a rope and harness for safety, but not as aid while climbing.

descend

To go down is to descend.

rating systems

Rating systems rate the difficulty and length of climbs. Difficulty is rated on a system of 5.0 through 5.15. Length is rated I through VI.

sling

A sling is a loop worn by a rock climber to carry protection and other equipment.

solo

Climbing solo means to climb alone, without help or protection.

quickdraw

A quickdraw is a piece of webbing with a carabiner at each end. It is used to link together pieces of protection.

smearing

In this technique, climbers place a large area of their shoes' soles on the rock. The pressure and rubber soles create enough grip to move upward.

sport climbing

Sport climbing is competition climbing focused on speed and the route.

spotter

A spotter is someone who watches over a climbing partner and is positioned to help in a fall.

traversing

To traverse is to climb sideways while making an ascent.

top roping

Top roping is a method of rigging the rope for belaying. The rope passes through an anchor at the top of the rock.

Famous Climbers

Many athletes have become famous for their rock climbing skills. Royal Robbins is known for achieving the first ascent of Yosemite National Park's Half Dome in 1957. Ron Kauk and John Bachar are known for their skill in free climbing. Yvon Chouinard is known for his ice-climbing skills. His **environmentally** friendly equipment designs are used in much of today's rock climbing.

Lynn Hill is one of the best-known female climbers. She started climbing in 1975, when she was 14 years old. At first, she practiced traditional climbing in areas such as Joshua Tree National Park and Yosemite National Park. She soon became known for her skill at climbing difficult routes.

In the mid-1980s, Hill visited France and discovered sport climbing. She competed and won in many events, including a co-win at the World Cup. In France in 1990, she became the first woman to complete a route rated 5.14. But Hill eventually gave up sport climbing to return to more traditional climbing.

Ron Kauk

In 1993, Hill and a climbing partner were the first to free climb a route called the Nose on Yosemite's El Capitan. They completed the climb in only four days. One of Hill's biggest accomplishments came a year later. She set a record by free climbing the same route in just 23 hours. Today, she continues to free climb rock walls around the world.

Rock Climbing Today

Traditional climbing is still practiced by many people. But other types of climbing are also popular. Today, climbers can try different styles, such as sport climbing, bouldering, and big wall climbing.

In sport climbing, the route is the focus, rather than reaching a summit. The climb can be either on outdoor **crags** or on indoor climbing walls. The climber ascends a planned route, clipping into protection devices already set in the wall. As a climber learns, he or she can try more difficult routes. In sport competitions, climbers are judged on speed, the smoothness of the climb, and the difficulty of the path.

Bouldering is a type of climbing done on small boulders or other areas of low rock. Usually, these areas are close to the ground. Climbers who boulder focus on difficult routes and moves. Some bouldering routes are only a few feet long, but they are very challenging. Climbers often fall while trying to solve these climbing puzzles. Most do not use ropes. But they will often wear rock shoes and use chalk, a crash pad, and a spotter.

Big wall climbing involves long routes. Sometimes these routes take many days to complete. Specialized gear is a large part of big wall climbing. Climbers often camp on a ledge during the night. If a ledge is not available, climbers can use hanging platforms.

Today's sport of rock climbing owes its creation to **mountaineering**. The sport has gradually changed. But climbers continue to enjoy the problem solving and **technique** that go into a climb. Often, their efforts are rewarded with a beautiful view from the summit.

Glossary

aluminum - a soft, silvery-white metal.

crag - a steep, rugged rock or cliff.

environment - all the surroundings that affect the growth and well-being of a living thing.

fiberglass - a material made of threads of glass.

flexible - able to bend without breaking.

momentum - the force of a moving object.

mountaineering - the sport of climbing mountains, which can involve rock climbing, ice climbing, and hiking. A person who does this is called a mountaineer.

nylon - a strong material that can stretch slightly.

surplus - an extra amount.

technique - the method used to perform an action or activity.

Web Sites

Would you like to learn more about rock climbing? Please visit **www.abdopub.com** to find up-to-date Web site links about this sport and its competitions. These links are routinely monitored and updated to provide the most current information available.

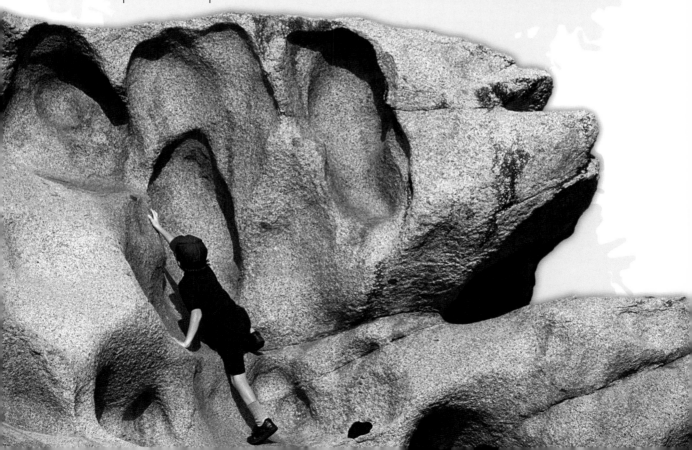

Index